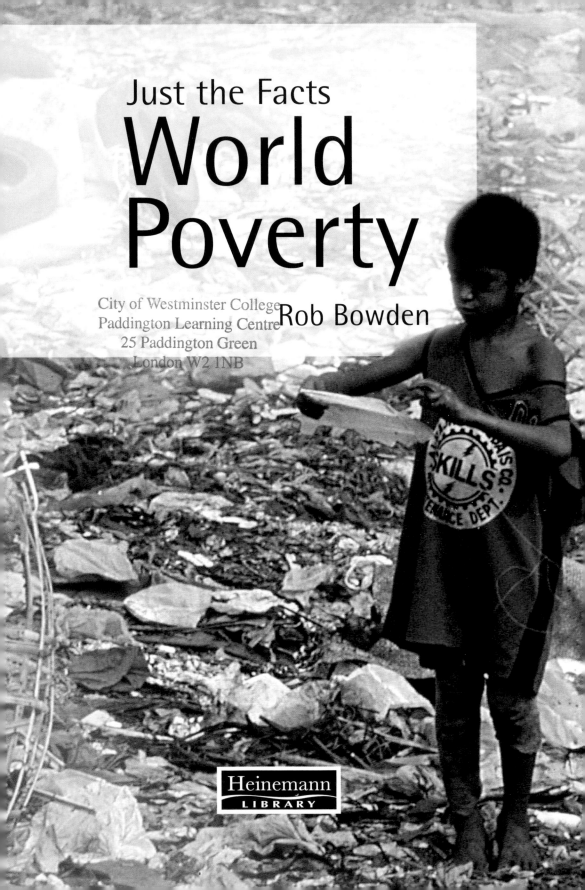

Just the Facts

World
Poverty

City of Westminster College
Paddington Learning Centre
25 Paddington Green
London W2 1NB

Rob Bowden

Heinemann
LIBRARY

www.heinemann.co.uk
Visit our website to find out more information about **Heinemann Library** books.

To order:
 Phone 44 (0) 1865 888066
 Send a fax to 44 (0) 1865 314091
Visit the Heinemann Bookshop at www.heinemann.co.uk to browse our catalogue and order online.

Produced by Monkey Puzzle Media Ltd, Gissing's Farm, Fressingfield, Suffolk IP21 5SH, UK

First published in Great Britain by Heinemann Library, Halley Court, Jordan Hill, Oxford OX2 8EJ, part of Harcourt Education. Heinemann is a registered trademark of Harcourt Education Ltd.

Editorial: Nick Hunter and Jennifer Tubbs
Series design: Mayer Media
Book design: Jane Hawkins
Production: Viv Hichens

Originated by Dot Gradations Ltd
Printed and bound in Hong Kong, China by South China Printers

ISBN 0 431 16142 9

06 05 04 03 02
10 9 8 7 6 5 4 3 2 1

British Library Cataloguing in Publication Data
Bowden, Rob
 World poverty. - (Just the facts)
 1.Poverty - Juvenile literature 2.Poverty -
 Developing countries - Juvenile literature
 I. Title
 339.4'6

Acknowledgements
The publishers would like to thank the following for permission to reproduce photographs:
Associated Press **38-39** (Keystone), **46**; Digital Vision **1**; Corbis **9**; Hulton Archive **8**, **10**; Hutchison Library **32** (Andrew Sole), **47** (Ian Lloyd), **48** (P Moszynski); Panos Pictures **14** (Giacomo Pirozzi), **18** (Sean Sprague), **19** (Sean Sprague), **24-25** (Liba Taylor), **28** (Jean-Leo Dugast), **31** (Trygve Bøstad); Popperfoto **35** (Reuters); Rex Features **45** (Today); Rob Bowden **23**; Still Pictures **6-7** (Franklin Hollander), **10-11** (Bojan Brecelj), **12-13** (Reinhard Janke), **15** (Mark Edwards), **16** (Mark Edwards), **20** bottom (David Hoffman), **20-21** (Ron Giling), **26-27** (Ron Giling), **27** (Jorgen Schytte), **29** (Hartmut Schwarzbach), **30-31** (John Isaac), **33** (Joerg Boethling), **34-35** (Ron Giling), **36-37** (Toby Adams), **40-41** (Shehzad Noorani), **42-43** (Ron Giling), **44** (Hartmut Schwarzbach); Topham Picturepoint **13** (Photri); UNHCR **4**.

Cover photograph reproduced with permission of Colin Jones/Impact.

Every effort has been made to contact copyright holders of any material reproduced in this book. Any omissions will be rectified in subsequent printings if notice is given to the publishers.

Any words appearing in the text in bold, **like this**, are explained in the Glossary.

Contents

Feeling poor

We have nearly all had the experience of feeling poor. You may have felt poor when you could not afford the latest CD or item of clothing, or perhaps when visiting someone better off than you and your family. But do these feelings mean you could say you were suffering from poverty? We all use words such as 'poor' and 'rich' in our everyday discussions, but without giving much thought to what they really mean.

Defining poverty

Poverty is usually measured by comparing people's incomes. People whose income is too low to meet basic needs, such as food and shelter or health and education, are said to be poor. This low level of income is known as a 'poverty line'. The amount of money necessary to meet basic needs varies from place to place, so each country has its own poverty line. In a very poor country such as Bangladesh, for example, it may be easy to meet basic needs with eleven US dollars (US$11) a day. In a wealthy country such as the USA, however, this would be very difficult – in fact, US$11 per day is used as the poverty line in the USA.

Rwandan refugees queue for water. The lack of such basic human needs is a sign of extreme poverty.

Such differences make it difficult to compare poverty between countries, so international measures of poverty have been developed as an alternative. The most widely used measure is the **international poverty line** (less than US$1 per day). Using this measure, an estimated 1.2 billion (1.2 thousand million) people – one in every five – began the 21st century living in poverty.

The **United Nations** (UN) and the **World Bank** also use a slightly higher poverty line of US$2 per day. Using this measure, the number of people living in poverty increases to 2.8 billion (2.8 thousand million) people and shows what a huge problem poverty is worldwide. Poverty is not just about income though, it is also about quality of life, such as being healthy or being able to read.

"Poverty is hunger. Poverty is lack of shelter. Poverty is being sick and not being able to see a doctor. Poverty is not being able to go to school and not knowing how to read. Poverty is not having a job, is fear for the future, living one day at a time. Poverty is losing a child to illness brought about by unclean water. Poverty is powerlessness, lack of representation and freedom."

(The World Bank's definition of poverty, 20 February 2001)

Degrees of poverty

Poverty lines tend to show those people living in 'absolute poverty', where they lack basic needs such as food, shelter and clothing. Absolute poverty can be measured by calculating the income required to meet those basic needs.

Relative poverty

Broader understandings of poverty introduce the more complicated idea of 'relative poverty'. This is where people are considered poor if their standard of living is significantly below normal for the country in which they live. For example, if you had no television while most of the people living around you did, then you could be considered relatively poor. You would be missing out on a normal part of your society's daily culture and enjoyment.

While access to a television may be of great importance to people living in Europe or North America, it would seem a minor concern to many of the poorest people in the world. They are more likely to be worried about the quality of their housing, or perhaps being able to afford a new pair of shoes, or soap for washing. This shows us that relative poverty, like absolute poverty, varies across regions and countries.

The map of poverty

On a global scale, poverty is found mainly in the countries of South Asia and sub-Saharan Africa. South Asia has the most people – 43.5 per cent of the world total – living below the international poverty line of US$1 per day. In sub-Saharan Africa, there are fewer people living below the international poverty line (24.3 per cent of the world total). But the proportion of people living in poverty in sub-Saharan Africa is the world's greatest (slightly more than 48 per cent). This means that almost half the population live on less than US$1 per day.

Other **less developed** regions, such as Latin America and the Caribbean, and East Asia, also have relatively high poverty levels, but in **more developed** (or 'industrialized') countries virtually no one lives below the international poverty line. However, poverty has been growing rapidly in the countries of Eastern Europe, where the number of people living on less than US$1 per day increased from 1.1 million in 1987 to 17.6 million by 1998. This makes Eastern Europe the fastest-growing region of poverty in the world.

In a more developed country such as Germany, children may think of themselves as poor if they do not have access to computer games.

Inequality and illiteracy

Accounts of poverty are found throughout history and also appear in literature from the past. For example, in many of his novels, such as *Oliver Twist* and *Bleak House*, the British author Charles Dickens wrote about poverty in Victorian England. In *Bleak House*, Dickens describes Jo, an **illiterate** boy living in London:

> **❝**It must be a strange state to be like Jo! To shuffle through the streets, unfamiliar with the shapes, and in utter darkness as to the meaning of those mysterious symbols, so abundant over the shops, and at the corners of streets, and on the doors, and in the windows! To see people read, and to see people write, and to see the postmen deliver letters, and not to have the least idea of all that language.**❞**

(From *Bleak House* by Charles Dickens, written in 1853)

The illiteracy that Dickens writes about is as much a feature of poverty today as it was in 1853. According to a **United Nations** report published in 2001, in the least developed countries in the world almost half of all people over the age of fifteen were illiterate in 1999. Historical writings on poverty also refer to the difference between the rich and the poor, or what is usually called '**inequality**'. Some simply described these inequalities; others discussed why they came about and how some people became rich at the expense of others. The account of an American slave, opposite, tells how his mother remained in poverty while her master benefited from her hard work.

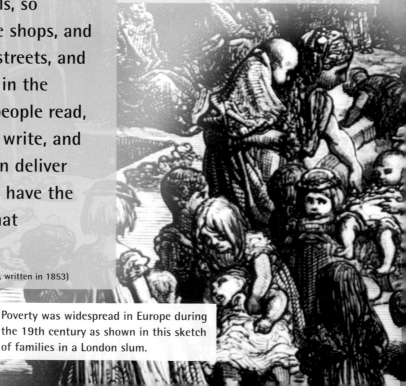

Poverty was widespread in Europe during the 19th century as shown in this sketch of families in a London slum.

Slaves, watched by their masters, operate machinery on a cotton plantation in southern America.

"I never saw my mother, to know her as such, more than four or five times in my life; and each of these times was very short in duration, and at night. She was hired by a Mr Stewart, who lived about twelve miles from my home. She made her journeys to see me in the night, travelling the whole distance on foot, after the performance of her day's work. She was a field hand, and a whipping is the penalty of not being in the field at sunrise, unless a slave has special permission from his or her master.**"**

(From *Narrative of the Life of Frederick Douglass, an American Slave*, 1845)

Colonialism

The poverty that exists today has developed as a result of **inequalities** and differences built up over time. Many individuals, countries and regions have grown wealthy at the expense of others. During the 19th century, European powers such as Britain, France, the Netherlands and Belgium gained control of large parts of the world. These areas were known as **colonies**, and they provided a wealth of **raw materials** and valuable products, for example, gold from South Africa, sugar cane from the Caribbean and tea from India. These were mined or harvested using a cheap and plentiful supply of local labour, and exported back to Europe where they were converted into manufactured goods and products.

In the early part of the 20th century, Dutch colonialists in Java, Indonesia enjoyed great wealth – unlike those who waited on them.

These goods were then sold at a much higher price. Many of them were sold to the colonies from which the raw materials had originally come. As this pattern repeated itself over time, the money flowed back to the European powers through the hands of rich merchants and trading companies.

Although the colonies became politically independent during the second half of the 20th century, many remain trapped by the inequalities that had been established. To make matters worse, during the last 60 years, businesses have taken the place of the colonial powers as the main traders in the modern economy. They show little loyalty to the countries with which they trade. They will bargain for the lowest possible prices, which means that sometimes suppliers can barely earn enough to survive. Recent years have seen a sharp fall in the price of the commodities (goods such as sugar, tea, cotton etc.) on which many of the poorest countries in the world rely. In the 1990s, commodity prices were 45 per cent lower than they were during the 1980s.

Today plantation workers prepare Jamaican Blue Mountain coffee for export to Europe and North America.

The gap widens

The unequal patterns of trade and exchange established in the past mean that the extremes of poverty and wealth have grown greater over time. In 1960, for example, the fifth of the world's population living in the wealthiest countries had an average income 30 times higher than the fifth of the world's population living in the very poorest countries. This had increased to 60 times higher by 1990, and had reached 74 times higher by 1998.

The rich-poor divide

More and more, global wealth is concentrated among a few privileged groups and individuals. For example, the richest 10 per cent of Americans (about 25 million people) enjoy a total income greater than that of the poorest 43 per cent of the world population (around two billion – two thousand million – people). More shocking still, the world's three richest people (including Bill Gates of Microsoft) have greater wealth than the population of the 43 least developed countries combined.

Inequalities are found within countries too. In Australia, for example, the richest 10 per cent of the population is 12.5 times better off than the poorest 10 per cent. In the USA, the richest 10 per cent is 16.6 times better off, and in Brazil 48.7 times! Such figures show that poverty is not just suffered by people living in Africa or Asia, as is often suggested by the media. It can be found in communities throughout the world. In 1999, for example, an estimated 12 million children were hungry (or at risk from hunger) in the world's wealthiest country, the USA.

A beggar outside a shopping mall in Germany shows that poverty is everywhere, even in wealthy countries.

❝No longer inevitable, poverty should be relegated to history along with slavery, colonialism and nuclear warfare.❞
(From the UNDP Human Development Report 1997)

Not all bad news!

While the figures may be shocking, it is important to realize that much has been achieved in tackling poverty. In fact, poverty has reduced more in the last 50 years than it did in the previous 500. Today more people are literate (able to read and write) than ever before, and we are living longer too. The world's population is healthier and better fed, and the quality of our living environment (homes and towns) has improved dramatically. However, many still suffer daily from the effects of poverty. This is a depressing fact, given that the **United Nations Development Programme (UNDP)**, one of the leaders in the fight against world poverty, argues that no one need suffer poverty in the 21st century. Many people believe that ridding the world of poverty would be a real possibility if wealth was spread more equally between everyone. This view is supported by the fact that just 1 per cent of the wealth of the 200 richest people in the world could provide primary education for all of the world's children. But in reality, as we shall see, poverty is a much more complex issue.

Reductions in poverty mean that people are living for longer than ever before. This North American couple enjoy a jog along the beach.

13

Quality of life

Although many of the ways of measuring poverty focus on income levels, poverty is about much more than money. Experts studying poverty began to realize that people continued to suffer the symptoms of poverty, such as hunger and poor health and education, even though their incomes increased. As a result, poverty experts started to look more closely at 'quality of life' measures like health and education.

The focus on income measures is known as the study of **income poverty**, while the focus on quality of life measures is the study of **human poverty**. These poverty measures are closely linked. If your parents have a good income, for example, it can help you to achieve a good education, which gives you a better chance of finding a well-paid job. Similarly, a low income may mean that you cannot afford basic healthcare and suffer from regular illness as a result. Such illness makes it difficult for you to work, the result of which is that you earn less. This **interdependence** between income and human poverty is called the cycle of poverty.

Education and skills can help to reduce poverty. This Rwandan woman is learning to use a computer.

The elderly are particularly vulnerable to poverty. This woman tries to keep warm during a cold London winter.

The reality of poverty

By reducing poverty to statistics, there is a danger that its harsh realities may be forgotten or ignored. The fact is that people in your own society and in societies throughout the world suffer the realities of poverty every day. You've probably seen signs of poverty for yourself, such as beggars asking for money to buy food, or homeless people sleeping in shop doorways. Other signs of poverty are less obvious, for example, the elderly pensioner huddled next to an electric fire because he or she cannot afford to heat their entire home.

Absolute poverty

The poverty experienced by people living in **less developed** countries is perhaps not immediately obvious to people living in **more developed** nations. In less developed countries, many of the poor do not even have enough food to keep themselves healthy and alive. For more than a billion (one thousand million) of them, the water they drink is contaminated with the **bacteria** or **parasites** responsible for killer illnesses. In 1998 just one of these illnesses, diarrhoea, killed an estimated 2.2 million people, nearly all of whom were poor.

India has some of the poorest slums in the world, such as here in Delhi.

The struggle to survive

The poor live in low-quality housing, often without services such as electricity and water. In many cases there is no waste disposal system. Rubbish is simply dumped near the home, where it attracts pests and vermin, or is burned, releasing choking, toxic fumes. If the poor can afford treatment for illness, the nearest health centre may be tens of kilometres away by foot and will probably lack medical supplies and trained staff. The children of the poor will be lucky to complete their primary schooling. The cost of fees means that some may never go to school. Those who do attend may be in classes of more than 80 children with no trained teacher and only a handful of books to share. If they survive their childhood, which many of the poorest children will not, they will have to work long hours in low-paid jobs if they are to earn enough for themselves and their families. The poor are often powerless to change their circumstances; they can only hope for a better life for their children. The poor die young, perhaps 20 to 30 years sooner than you or me.

The above description is a generalization of poverty. In reality, experiences of poverty vary both between, and within, places. This makes it difficult fully to understand poverty in society. To help with this problem, the **United Nations** has a range of measures to monitor changes in the health and education of a society. By looking at these, we can gain an impression of poverty at a global level.

Life expectancy

One of the simplest poverty measures is life expectancy. The contrasts are stark. In Japan, one of the world's wealthiest societies, people can expect to live for up to 81 years. In the poverty-stricken African countries of Mozambique, Rwanda and Sierra Leone, life expectancy is less than 40 years.

The provision of healthcare, education and basic facilities, such as clean water, all contribute to such contrasts in life expectancy. In Kenya, for example, where life expectancy is 51 years, there is only one doctor for every 6700 people. In Spain, where there is a doctor for every 250 people, life expectancy is 78 years.

Lack of access to medical care may mean a very short life for some of these children in Kenya.

Generally it appears that quality of life improves as income gets higher, which again suggests that income and human poverty are dependent on one another. However, there are some important exceptions to this rule. Sri Lanka, for example, with an average annual income (**GDP per capita**) of US$3279, has a life expectancy of 72 years, and almost 92 per cent of Sri Lankan adults are literate. Brazil has a higher GDP per capita at US$7037, yet its life expectancy is 67 years and adult literacy is 85 per cent – lower than that of Sri Lanka.

Cuba is another good example. Life expectancy in Cuba is 76, only one year less than in the USA, and adult literacy (97 per cent) is only 2 per cent lower. Yet Cuba's GDP per capita of US$3967 is far less than that of the USA, at US$29,605. These exceptions show that it is possible for countries to make great progress in tackling human poverty without having great wealth.

These Cuban children attending a health centre can expect to live long lives despite having low incomes.

Inequalities

Global poverty is calculated using averages. While this type of calculation is useful, it is also important to look at poverty within the individual societies. For example, poverty in rural areas is often higher than in urban areas. Higher levels of poverty among **ethnic minorities** and women are also common in most societies. Some of the differences can be quite dramatic.

Contrasts

In Uganda, for example, 57 per cent of the rural population lacks access to healthcare facilities compared with just 5 per cent in urban areas. In Jamaica, 92 per cent of the urban population has access to a safe water source, but in rural areas this falls to just 48 per cent. Such contrasts are not limited to **less developed** countries. In the UK, for instance, the minority Pakistani/Bangladeshi community is four times poorer than the majority white community. In the USA, around 22 per cent of the black and Hispanic communities are classed as poor, compared with just 7.5 per cent among the majority white community.

In the UK, single parents often suffer greater poverty than others in society in general.

Gender inequalities

Women make up a large number of the poor, 70 per cent worldwide. They often work in lower paid or part-time jobs, as they try to manage the burden of caring for their families. In the Netherlands or Brazil, for example, women earn less than half the average male wage, and in Pakistan or Peru they earn less than a third. Women also experience greater human poverty, and often from a very young age. In poor households, boys are often sent to school in preference to girls, whose education is less valued.

Improving women's education can help to raise the whole family out of poverty. A clear example of this is the decrease in child mortality figures (the number of children per 1000 who die before the age of five) as their mothers' education increases. In the mid-1990s in the Philippines, child mortality among children born to women with no education was 152 per 1000, but fell to 70 per 1000 for children born to women who had completed primary school, and 42 per 1000 for women with secondary education. Despite such dramatic evidence being repeated throughout the world, women remain especially poor, a fact which led the **United Nations** to state in 1995 that 'poverty has a woman's face'.

By learning to read, these Bangladeshi girls can hope for a better future.

21

Child poverty

Throughout the world, millions of children grow up living in poverty, without enough to eat or proper clothes. If they go to school, they are among the lucky ones. Millions of children do not even get to school, and instead find themselves working from as young as six years of age. Some of these working children have been well-publicized by the media, working in factories (known as sweat-shops) making clothes or stitching footballs or trainers. The vast majority of poor children work at home, however, helping out in the family fields or caring for younger children while their parents work. Take Betty, for example, a ten-year-old girl living on the shores of Lake Victoria in Uganda.

❝I am happy today, because tomorrow my sister comes home from school. She can help me with the work here; with looking after my three younger brothers and caring for the chickens and pig. Next week we will have to harvest the maize too and take it for grinding at the mill. My parents work at the lake where they cook food for the fishermen, but I must stay here and look after the home. That is why I can't go to school. I walk with my friends in the morning to collect water, but when they go to school I must come home to start work. I want to be a nurse when I grow up, but if I don't go to school, then it won't be possible. I can't even read or write properly.❞

(Betty Angatai, April 1999)

There are millions of children like Betty living in **less developed** countries. But child poverty is not limited to these regions. There are more than 4 million children living in poverty in the UK and more than 11 million in the USA. Most of these children experience a different form of poverty to that suffered by Betty, but their plight confirms poverty's universal nature.

Instead of being at school, Betty washes the dishes in water she has carried from a borehole more than 3 kilometres away.

Population and poverty

The debate about the causes of poverty has many sides, each with its own merits. Some of the arguments have existed for many years, others are newer and reflect the rapidly changing world in which we live. Poverty is a complex issue and sometimes it seems that the only thing people agree on is that they disagree! What is important is that people try to understand more about poverty. Let's consider some of the main arguments about its causes.

Overpopulation

One of the oldest arguments is that poverty is caused by overpopulation. In particular, this is used when poverty in **less developed** regions, such as Africa or Asia, is being discussed. The argument is that people are poor because there are too many of them and the population is expanding too rapidly. There is some evidence to support such beliefs. In **sub-Saharan Africa**, for example, the population expanded by 2.8 per cent each year between 1975 and 1999. This compares with a population growth rate of just 0.8 per cent in the **more developed** countries. Fertility – the average number of children born to each woman – is also higher in regions of greater poverty.

The population argument dates back to 1798 and the theories put forward by Thomas Malthus, a British economist. Malthus believed that population would increase faster than food supplies. During the 1960s and 1970s, such ideas were used to explain the growing poverty and terrible famines experienced by parts of the less developed world. The phrase 'population explosion' was used, and governments and international agencies set about trying to control population as a way of reducing poverty.

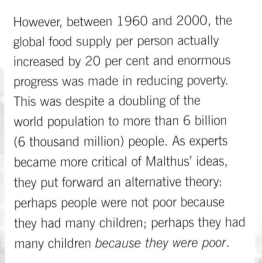

However, between 1960 and 2000, the global food supply per person actually increased by 20 per cent and enormous progress was made in reducing poverty. This was despite a doubling of the world population to more than 6 billion (6 thousand million) people. As experts became more critical of Malthus' ideas, they put forward an alternative theory: perhaps people were not poor because they had many children; perhaps they had many children *because they were poor*.

❝Fertility is highest in the poorest countries and among the poorest people in these countries. Failures in health, education and other services, especially for women, contribute to poverty in these countries.❞

(From a United Nations Population Fund (UNFPA) report entitled 'The State of World Population 2001')

Scenes, such as these of Rwandan refugees, often lead people to blame poverty on population growth. But the reality is much more complex.

The importance of children

Children born into poverty are less likely to survive. Parents therefore have more children than they would otherwise choose to ensure that some of them live to adulthood. Children are also valued for their contribution to the income of the poor. From as young as twelve years of age, children in **less developed** countries may contribute as much to the household income as an adult. Children also play an important role in caring for their parents when they become too old to work. This is especially the case in poor countries where there is little or no state support for the elderly. Those living in poverty often have lower education levels. This means that they may be less aware of the various methods of **contraception** available to limit the size of their families.

These children working on the maize harvest in rural Ghana make an important contribution to the income and survival of their families.

In 1974, the World Conference on Population indicated international support for these arguments. Experts pointed out that in countries where education and health services were available (especially to women), fertility levels declined swiftly. Rapid population growth, they said, was not a cause of poverty, but a symptom. (In other words, rapid population growth was a sign that people were poor and unable fully to control the size of their families.)

Global trade

Trade involves the flow of goods and services and the movement around the world of the money used to buy or sell them. Trade is closely related to wealth and poverty. It has increased significantly during the last 50 years and, as a result, has helped to reduce world poverty. But anti-poverty groups are cautious about the benefits of trade and argue that the current world trading system is not fair. They are concerned that, as trade increases further, poverty could grow. So who is right?

Vietnam uses its expertise in rice cultivation to compete in a global market.

27

Opening up to trade

Global trade is based on competition. Countries produce those goods and services that they can sell for a lower cost than their competitors. But the system only works if trade is free and equal. If individual countries limit free trade, then the system becomes corrupt and unfair. For this reason, countries are encouraged to open their economies to greater trading and remove any barriers, such as **tariffs** or **quotas** that affect the flow of goods and services.

Countries that have opened their economies to trade have experienced rapid economic growth. International companies have invested there and local industries have gained access to new global markets. The best examples are in East Asia, and include South Korea, Malaysia, Taiwan, China, Hong Kong and Singapore. These so-called 'Asian Tiger Economies' have also experienced some of the fastest declines in poverty ever known. So if they can achieve such success, why haven't other poor countries followed their example?

Singapore, one of the Asian Tigers, has used global trading successfully to reduce poverty.

The importance of investment

In truth, the success of the Asian Tigers in fighting poverty was achieved by more than simply opening up to greater trade. They also invested heavily in education to create a skilled workforce, and in healthcare to reduce the burden of disease. These factors are known to have an enormous impact on reducing poverty. So it was a package of measures that led to success, not trade alone. Many of the least developed (and poorest) countries do not have a skilled and healthy workforce with which to engage fully in world trade. They can only offer semi-skilled workers who tend to attract the lowest-paid jobs in the global economy. And, as countries compete to gain trade, they often reduce wages even further to make themselves more attractive (i.e. cheaper) to companies that might be considering investing in them.

Shanghai residents enjoy increasingly wealthy lifestyles as a result of rapid economic growth in China.

Overdependence

While free trade gives the poorest countries a fairer chance, it can also make them vulnerable to changes in the world economy. In many of the poorest countries, unskilled workers end up working long hours in appalling conditions for very little pay. Consumers benefit from cheaper goods – such as inexpensive T-shirts or jeans – made by people earning very low wages. Where poor countries have something to trade, it is often a **primary commodity** such as an agricultural product (coffee, tea, sugar, cocoa, rice etc.) or a mineral. Many poor countries are extremely dependent on these commodities. The problem is that these countries have little ability to control the price they receive for their produce, because prices are controlled by the world supply and demand. If there is high demand for a limited product then people will pay more, but if the product becomes more plentiful then the price falls. The earnings of these countries can therefore vary dramatically, making it hard for them to plan their development.

Countries, such as India, are extremely vulnerable to changing world prices for export crops like coffee.

Falling prices

Recently the prices of primary commodities such as grains and minerals have fallen – prices are now at their lowest level since 1850. At the same time, the prices of manufactured goods, such as tractors and cars, have risen. This creates problems for **less developed** countries: to buy the same number of cars or tractors, for example, they must sell an even greater amount of grain or minerals. But if they produce too much grain, the price they can charge for it falls even further. When only a little grain is available, producers can charge high prices, but when there is lots available the price comes down.

So poorer countries can become trapped in a cycle of producing more goods, but getting less money for them. Some countries are now producing **high-value commodities** as a way of overcoming this problem. In Kenya, for example, some farmers are switching to growing higher valued products, such as flowers, vegetables and herbs. This emerging industry is the fastest growing in Kenya. It has provided thousands of new jobs and helped local people escape poverty. But the initial investment for such projects is enormous, and many of the farms are owned by foreign companies, which means that the profits of this new trade go abroad.

High value products, such as flowers, are helping Kenya to reduce dependence on traditional export crops.

Globalization and poverty

The latest hope for relieving the world of poverty is **globalization**. This is a process by which global transport, travel and communications have developed very rapidly and become much cheaper. Such changes have led to enormous increases in trade, with producers now able to trade easily in new global markets using technology such as the Internet to sell their products. International organizations like the **World Bank** believe that globalization can make a big difference to poverty. They point out that, during the 1990s, the economies of **less developed** countries that took advantage of globalization grew in value by about 5 per cent per year, more than twice as fast as **more developed** countries. But globalization does not involve everyone.

Some 2 billion (2 thousand million) people have gained little or nothing from globalization. Many of them may never have made a telephone call, let alone used the Internet. Nearly all Internet use takes place in more developed countries. Critics of globalization fear that poverty may actually increase for many. As economies are forced to open up to greater trade, local producers may suddenly find that their products are no longer competitive, as somewhere else is able to produce them more cheaply. As a result, factories may reduce their workforces or **mechanize** their production to reduce costs. In some cases, factories may be forced to close altogether. Such changes lead to more unemployment and can force some people below the poverty line, unless they find alternative employment.

"Don't tell me about the global economy – half the people aren't part of it. What kind of economy leaves half the people behind?"

(Former US President Bill Clinton, the Dimbleby Lecture, BBC, 2001)

This abandoned textile mill in Bradford, UK, was once the world's largest. Today, imported textiles are cheaper than those produced in the UK.

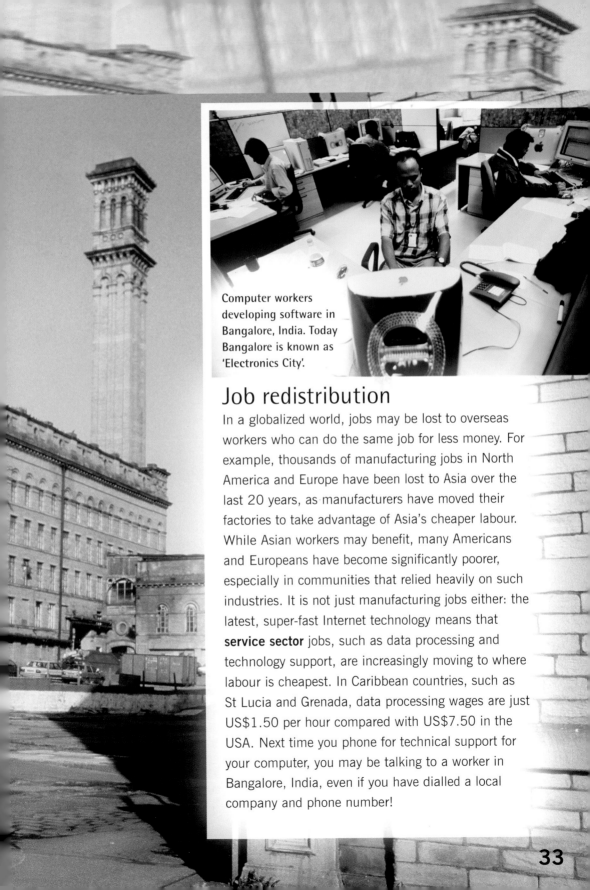

Computer workers developing software in Bangalore, India. Today Bangalore is known as 'Electronics City'.

Job redistribution

In a globalized world, jobs may be lost to overseas workers who can do the same job for less money. For example, thousands of manufacturing jobs in North America and Europe have been lost to Asia over the last 20 years, as manufacturers have moved their factories to take advantage of Asia's cheaper labour. While Asian workers may benefit, many Americans and Europeans have become significantly poorer, especially in communities that relied heavily on such industries. It is not just manufacturing jobs either: the latest, super-fast Internet technology means that **service sector** jobs, such as data processing and technology support, are increasingly moving to where labour is cheapest. In Caribbean countries, such as St Lucia and Grenada, data processing wages are just US$1.50 per hour compared with US$7.50 in the USA. Next time you phone for technical support for your computer, you may be talking to a worker in Bangalore, India, even if you have dialled a local company and phone number!

Transnational companies

Transnational companies (TNCs) are the major force in the global economy. In total, TNCs control around two-thirds of all world trade. The decisions made by TNCs, such as where in the world to locate their factories or offices can affect the well-being of millions of people worldwide. For those living on the edge of poverty, this can make **globalization** a very risky process.

TNCs are interested in making profits and will locate their production or purchase their supplies wherever is cheapest. Whole factories may be closed down if a TNC chooses to relocate. For semi-skilled workers this can mean a quick fall back into poverty. Experts suggest that only when people are able to survive such shocks can they really be said to have overcome poverty. Once above the **poverty** line, they should be able to stay there.

Making globalization work for the poor means that they need to have the same opportunities as those in wealthy nations. They must be educated and literate if they are to use the new technologies available but, more importantly, they must have access to markets in other countries.

Low paid female factory workers in southern India prepare clothing for export overseas.

European Union delegates meet in Beijing to discuss China's entry into the World Trade Organization.

The World Trade Organization

The World Trade Organization (WTO) was established in 1995 to regulate global trade. It sets rules that encourage free trading for all and penalizes those countries that break the rules. But less developed countries are under-represented at the WTO because they have fewer members to make decisions for them. This means that wealthy countries can shape agreements to their own advantage. In Europe, for example, a system of tariffs called the Common Agricultural Policy (CAP) limits the import of farm produce from outside Europe by taxing imports. This is extremely unfair to agricultural producers in other parts of the world.

If globalization is to work for the poor, then they need opportunities to trade on an equal basis. This would mean big changes to the way global trade is managed for those living in wealthy nations as well as those living in poverty. Farmers in Europe, for example, would have to run their businesses without the support of the Common Agricultural Policy.

Setting targets

In an effort to reduce poverty, the international community of countries has agreed several poverty-related targets to be met by the year 2015. Some of these are listed in the fact box below. Many of these targets look unlikely to be met. Even if they were, the world would still have several hundred million people living in extreme (absolute) poverty, and countless more living just above that.

International poverty-related targets
• To reduce the proportion of people living in extreme poverty by half between 1990 and 2015
• To enrol all children in primary school by 2015
• To provide equal access for boys and girls to primary and secondary education by 2005
• To reduce infant (under the age of one) and child (under the age of five) mortality rates by two thirds between 1990 and 2015.

(Source: Report by UN and other agencies, 'A Better World For All', 2000)

Workers build a new school in the Sudan. In the late 1990s just 53 per cent of Sudanese children were enrolled in primary school.

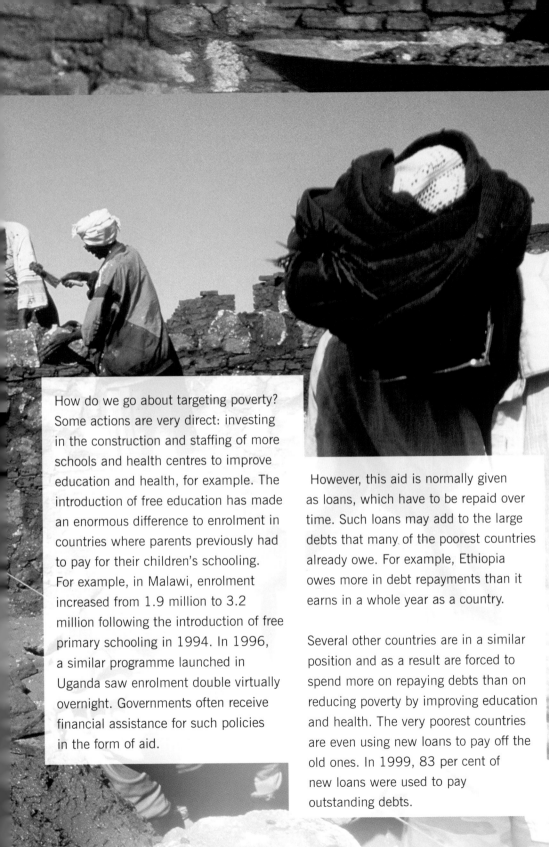

How do we go about targeting poverty? Some actions are very direct: investing in the construction and staffing of more schools and health centres to improve education and health, for example. The introduction of free education has made an enormous difference to enrolment in countries where parents previously had to pay for their children's schooling. For example, in Malawi, enrolment increased from 1.9 million to 3.2 million following the introduction of free primary schooling in 1994. In 1996, a similar programme launched in Uganda saw enrolment double virtually overnight. Governments often receive financial assistance for such policies in the form of aid.

However, this aid is normally given as loans, which have to be repaid over time. Such loans may add to the large debts that many of the poorest countries already owe. For example, Ethiopia owes more in debt repayments than it earns in a whole year as a country.

Several other countries are in a similar position and as a result are forced to spend more on repaying debts than on reducing poverty by improving education and health. The very poorest countries are even using new loans to pay off the old ones. In 1999, 83 per cent of new loans were used to pay outstanding debts.

37

The debt issue

Many campaigners against poverty believe that an effective way to relieve poverty would be to write off (cancel) the debts of poor countries. If debts were forgiven, they argue, then more money would be available to invest in local development. But writing off debts is not that simple. If countries do not pay back what they have already borrowed, then it means less may be available for future loans to other countries that need help. A scheme called the Heavily Indebted Poor Countries initiative (HIPC) has been launched as a possible solution to this problem.

HIPC looks at the debts of the poorest countries and aims to reduce them to a level at which the government can afford to make repayments, without having to cut back on its investment in development projects and poverty reduction. This is known as 'debt sustainability'. The HIPC also ensures that aid agencies and banks still receive sufficient repayments to continue providing new aid where it is needed. By September 2001, 23 countries were receiving debt relief worth a total of some US$34 billion ($34 thousand million) under the HIPC initiative. Almost all of these countries were in **sub-Saharan Africa**. Bolivia, Guyana, Honduras and Nicaragua in Central and South America were among the exceptions.

The 'Jubilee 2000' campaign (now 'Jubilee Plus') protests to put pressure on governments to write-off the debts owed by less developed countries.

Prioritizing poverty!

If poverty targets are to be met, then poverty has to be given higher priority. Governments need to focus spending on areas that are known to help reduce poverty, for example health and education. Aid for the poorest communities and countries must also be increased. At present the main aid-giving countries (the **more developed** countries) spend almost ten times more on military activity than they do on aid. The **United Nations** agreed that aid-giving nations should aim to give 0.7 per cent of their annual income to aid, but in 1999 only four countries – Denmark, Norway, the Netherlands and Sweden – achieved this target. Japan gave 0.35 per cent, Australia 0.26 per cent, the UK 0.23 per cent, and the USA (the world's richest country) only 0.1 per cent of its income.

If global poverty is to be ended, poorer countries need more financial help from richer ones. But the financial help decreases year by year. Between 1960 and 2000, the average person's income in the main aid-giving countries increased by US$16,000, but aid contributions increased by just US$3 per person.

Poverty initiatives

Providing aid benefits the poor, but it can also make people come to rely on money from elsewhere. Experts believe that it is more effective to improve people's ability to overcome and resist poverty for themselves. People often have their own ideas for dealing with poverty, but lack the initial investment required to put their ideas into practice. In recent years, poverty initiatives have been started to try to solve this problem.

Micro-credit schemes (small business loans) are one of the most successful initiatives. These schemes offer loans to people who are too poor to borrow money from normal banks. The loans are used to set up businesses, or improve existing ones, and are repaid as people begin to make a profit. Since the first scheme started in 1976, 'micro-credit' has spread to some 50 countries and helps more than 8 million individuals. It is hoped that 100 million people could benefit by 2005.

Members of the Grameen Bank repay their loans at a weekly meeting in Bangladesh.

The Grameen Bank

The Grameen Bank in Bangladesh was the first major micro-credit scheme. Started in 1976, with a loan of just US$27 to 42 workers, the Grameen Bank today loans around US$190 million per year to almost 2.4 million members. Women make up 94 per cent of the Bank's members, who are normally the poorest in society. Research tells us that women invest more of their income in their children and families, thus helping the next generation avoid poverty. A third of Grameen's members has been lifted out of poverty, and another third is about to cross the **poverty line**. The members' sense of motivation has led to new projects such as savings schemes and a mobile telephone network. An Internet service is being developed. All of these aim to help people to help themselves out of poverty. The founder of the Grameen Bank, Muhammad Yunus, believes very strongly that such simple strategies can work. As he says, 'these millions of small people with their millions of small pursuits can add up to create the biggest development wonder.'

Micro-credit schemes are even being used to tackle poverty in more developed countries. In the USA, for example, some 150,000 people living in deprived inner cities such as Chicago or Washington have benefited. A great strength of micro-credit is that it not only provides immediate relief from poverty, but also helps people to gain a sense of pride and achievement and encourages them to help themselves and their families in other ways. In short, it makes them realize that they do not have to be victims of poverty – they can do something about it.

Food for work

Other poverty initiatives involve schemes in which benefits are exchanged. 'Food for work' programmes are an example of this. Poor people work on projects, such as road building or environmental management, and are in turn provided with food for their labour. Some experts have criticized these schemes for providing only short-term help and failing to give people the skills they need to stay out of poverty. But supporters say food for work programmes are beneficial because they ensure that poor people receive a nutritious meal and the fact that they are working contributes to long-term development.

Building a dam in Ethiopia – these workers will each receive 6 kilos of grain in return for 6 hours work.

"Here in Australia, a number of vendors have used the *Big Issue* to get back on their feet, using the income they've earned to get out of emergency accommodation, for instance, or to move back into the mainstream work force."

(The *Big Issue* Australia website, 2002)

One successful exchange scheme is that of magazines, such as the *Big Issue*. Homeless or long-term unemployed people living in poverty purchase copies of these magazines from the publisher. They then sell them on to the general public for twice the price. The profit helps people living in poverty to plan for their future.

Poverty charities

One of the more obvious ways in which we see something being done about poverty is through various charities that specialize in helping those afflicted by it. Oxfam is one of the best known and has been fighting poverty for more than 50 years. Oxfam raises funds through collections, sponsored events and sales of goods in its stores. It uses this money to invest in projects for the poor, such as helping people to set up small businesses or funding new school buildings. Oxfam operates on a global level, but many charities focus on poverty at a more local level, in our own neighbourhoods. There are hundreds of poverty charities and they are often looking for volunteers to help raise funds, so it is one way that people can make a real difference.

Experiencing poverty

Most people reading this book will live in a **more developed** country. This means that, in global terms, they are unlikely to be poor. However, as mentioned before, people can be relatively poor if their quality of life and income are below the average for the country in which they live. In the USA, for example, they may be unable to afford health insurance, or to pay subscription or licence fees to enjoy television. But what about those whose quality of life and income are above average for their country? How do they experience poverty? It might not be obvious, but these people probably come into contact with poverty more than they think. They may, for example, have seen homeless people asking for help on the local high street. They have probably donated clothes, shoes or other goods to local charities at some time in their lives. These items are sold on by the charities to raise money to assist less fortunate members of society.

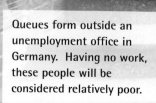

Queues form outside an unemployment office in Germany. Having no work, these people will be considered relatively poor.

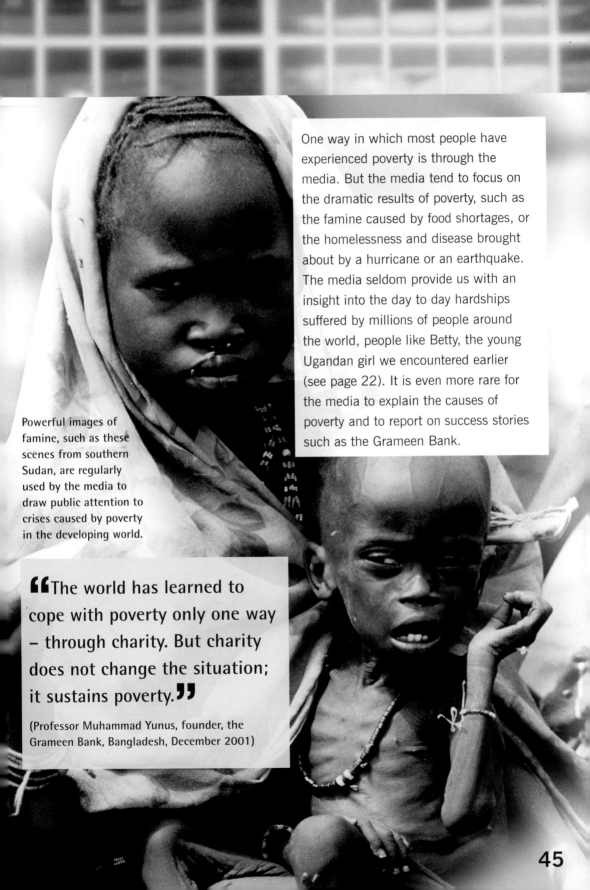

One way in which most people have experienced poverty is through the media. But the media tend to focus on the dramatic results of poverty, such as the famine caused by food shortages, or the homelessness and disease brought about by a hurricane or an earthquake. The media seldom provide us with an insight into the day to day hardships suffered by millions of people around the world, people like Betty, the young Ugandan girl we encountered earlier (see page 22). It is even more rare for the media to explain the causes of poverty and to report on success stories such as the Grameen Bank.

Powerful images of famine, such as these scenes from southern Sudan, are regularly used by the media to draw public attention to crises caused by poverty in the developing world.

❝The world has learned to cope with poverty only one way – through charity. But charity does not change the situation; it sustains poverty.❞

(Professor Muhammad Yunus, founder, the Grameen Bank, Bangladesh, December 2001)

Protection against poverty

In most developed countries there are systems to protect people against the effects of extreme poverty. If a person is unable to afford a place to live or enough food to eat, then the government will normally give him or her money to help. But, in the same way that countries can become dependent on aid, individuals can come to rely on benefits. In the USA, evidence suggests that dependency on the **welfare system** has increased over the last 30 years and is even passed on to the next generation.

An unemployed American searches for a new job assisted by a job counsellor.

The concern is that this 'intergenerational dependency' is now about much more than material poverty. It is about spiritual poverty – a feeling of hopelessness and exclusion.

Intergenerational dependency is experienced in most countries and is closely related to the cycles of poverty mentioned earlier. To combat this problem, governments are now targeting their anti-poverty schemes at giving people the skills and confidence to provide for themselves. But some vulnerable groups still need direct assistance. Single parents, for example, may be unable to work unless they receive help in caring for their children.

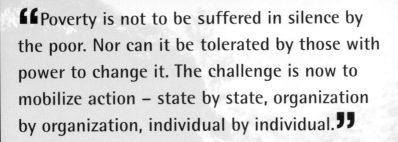

"Poverty is not to be suffered in silence by the poor. Nor can it be tolerated by those with power to change it. The challenge is now to mobilize action – state by state, organization by organization, individual by individual."

(James Gustave Speth, administrator of the United Nations Development Programme (UNDP) from 1993-1999)

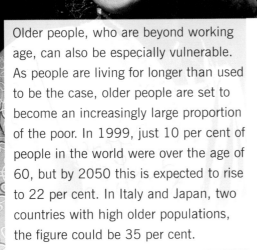

Older people, who are beyond working age, can also be especially vulnerable. As people are living for longer than used to be the case, older people are set to become an increasingly large proportion of the poor. In 1999, just 10 per cent of people in the world were over the age of 60, but by 2050 this is expected to rise to 22 per cent. In Italy and Japan, two countries with high older populations, the figure could be 35 per cent.

Support from families and neighbours can help relieve poverty for the elderly and other vulnerable groups.

In countries where the government is unable to provide full welfare support, protection of the poor and elderly often relies on assistance from family members or the community. But many of these support systems are breaking down. Young people move away from home in search of jobs and are no longer able to care for their elderly relatives. Many neighbourhoods are simply a collection of strangers, where people are unlikely to assist one another in times of poverty.

Action against poverty

We can all take action against poverty. By educating ourselves and learning as many skills as possible, we can ensure that we have a better chance of finding employment. Saving money, instead of spending it, is also a simple method of providing some protection against poverty. However, if everyone saved their money instead of purchasing goods and services, then those providing such goods could be put out of business and find themselves in poverty. We can also act against world poverty in more direct ways. Some people give money to the organizations that fund projects and campaigns to reduce poverty, such as Oxfam, ActionAid or Save the Children. Others help by doing voluntary work for these charities.

We can also influence poverty by simple changes to our behaviour. Recycling unwanted clothes instead of throwing them away is one example. Donating clothes to charity means that they can be purchased for a relatively low price by a person with less money, who will then be able to use their cash for something other than clothing. Look in shops for products that have been traded fairly. The packaging of these products will usually have a statement written on it to confirm that the producers have been paid a fair price and work in good conditions. If people buy locally from independent shops, they can also help to reduce or prevent poverty in their own communities.

Voluntary aid workers join a local development project in Somalia. The best results will be achieved by working together.

Fair trade

The number of fair trade products available in supermarkets and shops is increasing rapidly. Tea, coffee, bananas, chocolate, rice, sugar and honey are among some of the more commonly available items. The fair trade system supports small-scale producers (these are often producers who use only family labour) in selling and marketing their produce. Fair trade buyers agree a price with the producer that is guaranteed, no matter how the world price varies. This means the producer can plan ahead, knowing what their income will be. One of the greatest benefits, however, is not the guaranteed price, but the fact that they are paid half of the money in advance. This means that the producers can avoid borrowing money from banks or lenders and going into debt. It also means that they receive their incomes throughout the year, not just as one lump sum at harvest time.

The fair trade system offers producers some stability in their lives and businesses. This means that they can invest in the health, education and well-being of their families. Many have also developed new businesses or managed to start saving. It is easy to identify fair trade products by their logo, so next time you go shopping think about buying fairly and taking your own action against poverty.

Poverty awareness

Perhaps the greatest contribution we can make to reducing poverty is to increase our awareness of its presence and its causes. Most of the world's poor suffer poverty with little choice, but they do not suffer idly. Given the opportunities, poor people have many ideas and are determined to climb out of poverty. The key to eradicating poverty in the 21st century is to give them those opportunities. Better awareness is a vital first step.

A selection of Fairtrade products. Keep a look out for them at your local supermarket. The Fairtrade logo identifies items bought from small-scale producers working for a fair price.

"We believe that poverty does not belong to a civilized human society. It belongs to museums."
(Professor Muhammad Yunus, founder, the Grameen Bank, December 2001)

Facts and figures

Poverty forces this young child to scavenge discarded waste from a dump in Jakarta, Indonesia.

The change in population living on under US$1 per day (1987–98)

Region	1987 millions	1987 % total population	1998 millions	1998 % total population
Middle East and N. Africa	9.3	4.3	6.0	2.1
E. Asia and Pacific	417.5	26.6	267.1	14.7
Latin America and Caribbean	63.7	15.3	60.7	12.1
S. Asia	474.4	44.9	521.8	40.0
Sub-Saharan Africa	217.2	46.6	301.6	48.1
E. Europe and Central Asia	1.1	0.2	17.6	3.7

Source : World Bank Poverty Net

The percentage of the population living on under US$1 per day in **less developed** countries (1999)

Country	Percentage (%)	Country	Percentage (%)
Brazil	9.0	Indonesia	7.7
China	18.5	India	44.2
Kenya	26.5	Ghana	38.8
South Africa	11.5	Thailand	less than 2.0
Bangladesh	29.1	Jordan	less than 2.0
Mexico	12.2	Jamaica	3.2

Source : United Nations Human Development Report 2001

US$1 per day = the international poverty line

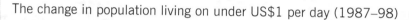

The percentage of the population living on under US$11 per day
in **more developed** countries (1994–5)

Country	Percentage (%)	Country	Percentage (%)
UK	16	France	10
USA	14	Norway	4
Australia	12	Canada	7

Source : United Nations Human Development Report 2001

US$11 per day = US national poverty line

Figures for life expectancy, literacy, school enrolment and average income
in different regions of the world

Region of the world	Life expectancy at birth (in years)	Adult literacy (%)	Proportion of children* enrolled in school (%)	Average income GDP per capita (US$)
Arab states	66.4	61.3	63	4550
E. Asia and Pacific	69.2	85.3	71	3950
Latin America and Caribbean	69.6	87.8	74	6880
S. Asia	62.5	55.1	53	2280
Sub-Saharan Africa	48.8	59.6	42	1640
E. Europe and Central Asia	68.5	98.6	77	6290
Industrialized countries	76.6	97.5	87	22,020
World	66.7	79.2	65	6980

Source : United Nations Human Development Report 2001   * of school age

Further information

Contacts in the UK

ActionAid
Hamlyn House,
Macdonald Road,
London N19 5PG
Tel: 020 7561 7561
email: mail@actionaid.org.uk
http://www.actionaid.org

The *Big Issue*
236–240 Pentonville Road,
London N1 9JY
Tel: 020 7526 3200
email: editorial@bigissue.com
http://www.bigissue.com

Department For International Development (DFID)
Abercrombie House,
Eaglesham Road,
East Kilbride,
Glasgow G75 8EA
Tel: 01 355 84 3132
0845 300 4100 (if calling from within the UK)
email: enquiry@dfid.gov.uk
http://www.dfid.gov.uk

The Fairtrade Foundation
Suite 204,
16 Baldwin's Gardens,
London EC1N 7RJ
Tel: 020 7405 5942
email: mail@fairtrade.org.uk
http://www.fairtrade.org.uk

Jubilee Plus
Jubilee Research,
New Economics Foundation,
Cinnamon House,
6–8 Cole Street,
London SE1 4YH
Tel: 020 7089 2853
email: info.jubilee@neweconomics.org
http://www.jubileeplus.org

Oxfam
274 Banbury Road,
Oxford OX2 7DZ
Tel: 01865 311 311
email: oxfam@oxfam.org.uk
http://www.oxfam.org.uk

Contacts in the USA

ActionAid USA
1112 16th Street NW,
Suite 540,
Washington, D.C. 20036-4823
Tel: (1) 202 835 1240
email: office@actionaidusa.org
http://www.actionaid.org

The *Big Issue* LA
640 Venice Boulevard,
PMB 130,
Venice,
CA 90291
Tel: (1) 310 306 5712
http://www.bigissue.com/lafound.html

Oxfam America
26 West Street,
Boston.
MA 02111 1206
Tel: (1) 617 482 1211
email: info@oxfamamerica.org
http://www.oxfamamerica.org

Transfair USA
1611 Telegraph Avenue,
Suite 900,
Oakland, CA 94612
Tel: (1) 510 663 5260
email: transfair@transfairusa.org
http://www.transfairusa.org

United Nations Schools Site
Global Teaching and Learning Project,
C/o Cyberschoolbus,
One United Nations Plaza,
Room DC1-552,
New York, NY 10017
Tel: (1) 212 963 8589
email: cyberschoolbus@un.org
http://www.un.org/cyberschoolbus

**The United States Agency for International
Development (USAID)**
US Agency for International Development Center,
Ronald Reagan Building,
Washington, D.C. 20523-1000
Tel: (1) 202 712 4810
email: inquiries@usaid.gov
http://www.usaid.gov

World Bank Poverty Net
1818 H Street, NW,
Washington, D.C. 20433
Tel: (1) 202 473 1000
email: povertynet@worldbank.org
http://www.worldbank.org/poverty/

Contacts in Australia

Australian Bureau of Statistics
Locked Bag 10,
Belconnen ACT 2616
Tel: (61) 2 9268 4909
email: client.services@abc.gov.au
http://www.abs.gov.au

Australian Council of Social Service
Locked Bag 4777,
Strawberry Hills NSW 2012
Tel: (61) 2 9310 4844
email: acoss@acoss.org.au
http://www.acoss.org.au

The *Big Issue* Australia
GPO Box 4911V,
Melbourne 3001
Tel: (61) 3 9663 4522
email: bigissue@infoxchange.net.au
http://www.bigissue.org.au

Oxfam Community Aid Abroad
156 George Street, Fitzroy,
Melbourne 3065
Tel: (61) 3 9289 9444
email: enquire@caa.org.au
http://www.caa.org.au

Contacts in New Zealand

Oxfam New Zealand
Level 1, 62 Aitken Terrace,
Kingsland, Auckland 1032
Tel: (+64) 9 355 6500
email: oxfam@oxfam.org.nz
http://www.oxfam.org.nz

Contacts in Bangladesh

The Grameen Bank
Grameen Bank Bhaban, Mirpur,
Section-2, Dhaka-1216
Tel: 8802-9005257-68
email: grameen.bank@grameen.net
http://www.grameen-info.org

Disclaimer
All the Internet addresses (URLs) given in this
book were valid at the time of going to press.
However, due to the dynamic nature of the
Internet, some addresses may have changed, or
sites may have changed or ceased to exist since
publication. While the author and Publisher regret
any inconvenience this may cause readers, no
responsibility for any such changes can be
accepted by either the author or the Publisher.

Glossary

absolute poverty
inability to meet the basic needs such as food, shelter and clothing necessary for survival

bacteria
micro-organisms which contaminate food and water, causing infection and illness

colony
country occupied and ruled by a foreign country. For example, Kenya was a colony of Britain.

contraception
also called birth control. The prevention of unwanted pregnancy.

ethnic minorities
ethnic groups other than those that make up the majority of society

GDP
Gross Domestic Product (GDP) is the monetary value of goods and services produced by a country in a single year. Often measured per person (capita) as GDP per capita.

globalization
term used to describe the increased connections between different parts of the world through the speed up of communications (for example, via the internet) and greater international trade

high-value commodity
product that has a high value for international trading

human poverty
used to describe the conditions of the poor that can't be measured in terms of money, for example, illiteracy, poor health, and lack of security

illiterate
unable to read or write

income poverty
state of being poor according to the amount of income earned. Countries may have different levels of income poverty according to the cost of living in each place.

inequality
situation whereby income, resources, quality of life and opportunities (such as schooling) are not shared equally among a population. Inequality is found globally, nationally and locally.

interdependence
where two or more factors depend on one another

international poverty line
level of income used to measure poverty internationally for the purpose of global comparisons. The levels normally used are those with daily incomes below US$1 and US$2.

less developed world
poorer countries of the world (sometimes called the Third World), including most of Africa, Asia, Latin America and Oceania. People living there are often unhealthy, poorly educated and work in agriculture and low technology industries.

mechanize
equip a factory or industry with machinery, often resulting in a reduced need for human labour

micro-credit
sometimes known as 'micro-finance', micro-credit consists of small loans given to individuals or groups to help them start businesses or other income-generating schemes

more developed world

wealthier countries of the world, including Europe, North America, Japan, Australia and New Zealand. People living there are normally healthy, well educated and work in a wide variety of high technology industries.

national poverty line

level of income within a specific country below which people are considered to be poor. In the USA, for example, the level of US$11 per day is used.

parasites

organisms that live on or in other plants and animals. They can often cause infections or harm to their hosts.

primary commodity

product originating from nature, such as a mineral or agricultural good. It remains a primary commodity until it is processed or manufactured in some way.

quota

maximum quantity of goods which can be imported or exported. Quotas are usually set by governments and must not be exceeded.

raw materials

natural, unprocessed materials that are manufactured into finished goods

relative poverty

state of poverty in which a person is unable to enjoy the normal standard of living for the society in which he or she lives. In the UK or USA, for example, a person may be considered relatively poor if he or she cannot afford a television.

service sector

area of business that is responsible for providing an economy or population with services, e.g. communications, financial, commercial and educational

sub-Saharan Africa

geographical area including the countries in Africa south of the Sahara desert. It includes a total of 44 countries.

tariff

tax, set by governments, which must be paid when goods are imported from another country

transnational company (TNC)

major business that has offices, factories or investments in at least two countries. These are sometimes called multi-national companies (MNCs).

United Nations

group of independent nations that has united to promote international peace, co-operation and security. The UN was formed in 1945 and currently has 184 members.

welfare system

system of services and financial assistance provided by the government to help people meet their basic needs

World Bank

international bank set up in 1944 to promote economic development and growth. The World Bank funds projects by giving loans to its 178 member countries.

Index